W9-BGY-988

PEARLS FROM HEAVEN

Your Heavenly Father's Words of Love and Comfort

mary grace birkhead

Design by Brand Navigation
Bill Chiaravalle, DeAnna Pierce,
Russ McIntosh & Brittany Gerwig

INTEGRITY®
PUBLISHERS
Nashville

PEARLS FROM HEAVEN

Copyright © 2006 by Mary Grace Birkhead

Published by Integrity Publishers, a division of Integrity Media, Inc., 5250 Virginia Way, Suite 110, Brentwood, Tennessee 37027

All rights reserved. No portion of this publication may be reproduced, stored in a retrieval system or transmitted in any form by any means—electronic, mechanical, photocopying, recording, or any other—except for brief quotations in printed reviews, without the prior written permission of the publisher.

Unless otherwise indicated, Scripture quotations are taken from *The Holy Bible*, New International Version (NIV), copyright © 1973, 1978, 1984, International Bible Society. Used by permission of Zondervan Bible Publishers.

Cover and interior design: Brand Navigation, LLC, www.brandnavigation.com

ISBN 1-59145-494-8

Printed in the United States of America
06 07 08 09 10 LBM 6 5 4 3 2 1

THIS BOOK IS DEDICATED TO MY PARENTS,

FRANK & JOAN PENNINGTON,

WHO LOVE ME WITH SUCH UNCONDITIONAL LOVE.

I LOVE YOU.

Thank you to my husband, Rob, who shares with me in the adventure of finding "pearls." To my dear children Robert, Daniel, and Camille, who are my "pearls of great price." To the people who remind me of who and whose I am: Trisha McDermott, Sarah Young, Melinda Seibert, Roseanne Coleman, Tiffany Foss, Mary Trapnell, Susan Lipson, Julie Ward, "The Fabulous 40" Bible study leaders, and my pastors, Lloyd Shadrach and Jeff Schulte. Also the brave people at Integrity Publishers for believing in these books: Byron Williamson, Mark Gilroy, Barb James, Betty Woodmancy, Dale Wilstermann, and Joey Paul. And special thanks to Bill Chiaravalle, DeAnna Pierce, Russ McIntosh, and Brittany Gerwig for making this book so beautiful.

INTRODUCTION

Pearls are miracles. They are made over time under very special conditions.

Pearls are precious. They are priced at a premium for their uniqueness.

Pearls are discoveries. They are embedded in a shell underwater waiting to be uncovered.

Pearls are rare. They are celebrated when they are found.

They don't form in groups like peas. And unlike diamonds, they are solitary—not hewn off something larger. They are individually unique.

Traditionally, they are the gift of choice from the bridegroom to his bride.

God's Word is filled with "pearls." He has them waiting for you. They are unique; each one has something very specific about you. His pearls for you are priceless; they contain all truth and all wisdom. He longs for you to have them, string them together, and wear them close. Gather them and adorn yourself with His power, His desire, His truth, His passionate love, His promises, His faithfulness, His unwavering acceptance—all for you!

Pearls become more lustrous and colorful the longer they are worn. Unlike many things of this world that wear out, pearls richen with age. The natural oil in your skin brings out the true quality of the pearl. So, the closer you wear them and the longer you hold them the more beauty they will reveal.

God's pearls—His promises found in the Bible—are just like that. The more time you spend meditating on them, the more they will bless you. Unlike what the world offers, God's truths are eternal, not temporary fixes. His Words are refreshing and filled with life. God's Word is full of pearls; would you like to try on a strand?

You are a child of the King.

You are His beloved daughter.

He wants you to be in His presence.

He calls to you.

Bring all your hopes, longings, sorrows, and cares and lay them at His feet.

You are welcome in the throne room!

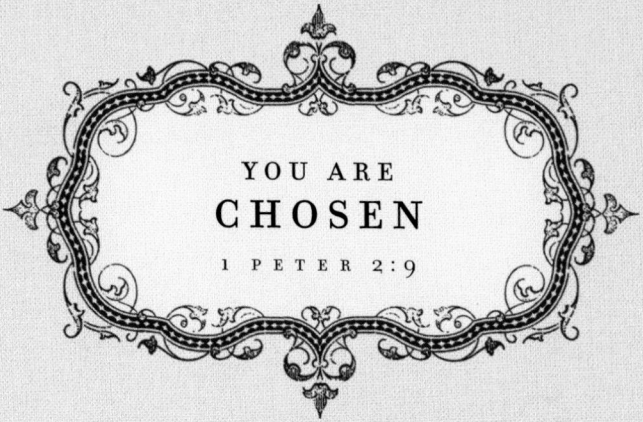

You are called out of darkness into His marvelous light.

You show forth His praises.

He lives in you and shines out of you.

You are filled with His power and light.

You are no longer a slave,

but an heir of the King!

Hallelujah!

Your soul will be satisfied with God's goodness.

He will sustain you, no matter the situation.

He will pour into you as you are poured out.

You won't run empty.

Don't trust in your strength, trust His.

There is no end to His goodness!

You don't need to carry a burden.

He wants you to have a light load.

Take every thought captive.

Hold each worry up to His light.

He is able to lift the weight off you.

Cast your cares on Him. He cares for you.

So unpack your heavy bags and rest!

You are becoming strong as you wait on the Lord.

He will give you the strength to hold on.

He is not weak. He won't let you fall.

He will provide your foot with

a firm place to stand.

He won't be late. He is trustworthy.

Help is on the way!

You will be comforted on sad days.

God will console your heart. He can give you what you need for the moment. He is able to redeem what has been taken away. He sees your tears and sadness. He desires to turn your sorrow into joy!

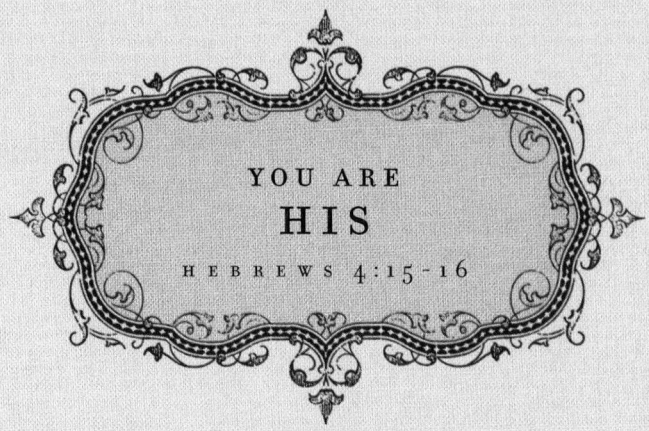

You have a God that knows all your weaknesses and needs.

He's walked in your shoes. He knows it's hard! He delights to show you mercy and give you grace. He has compassion on you and sees your heart.

Your need is not looked down on by Him. You are His beloved child.

Your faith pleases God.

He enjoys your trust in Him.

Your prayers are heard.

Your courage brings Him honor.

He sees your small, unseen sacrifices.

You're doing a great job. Keep trusting!

Your spirit will be supplied with good things.

His loving kindness is better than life.

He is the Giver of all good things.

He serves you from His banquet table.

What He provides is eternal

and perfect for you.

Praise Him with joyful lips!

You are equipped with all you need today.

God has gone out before you.

You are secure in His protection.

You won't be left with nothing.

God gives out of His abundance.

God is never surprised!

You are a well-watered garden.

God keeps watch over you.
Turn your face to His beautiful light.
He will continue to pour life into you.
Your dry soil can
be saturated with His lavish Spirit.
Bask in the warmth
of His immeasurable grace.

You don't have to be anxious.

God will give you peace.

He is a God of details.

He will surround you with comfort.

His all-seeing Spirit is actively working on your behalf.

Pray and receive what He has for you!

Your prayers are heard by God.

Your prayer is an act of faith.

Nothing is impossible with Him.

He will rescue you and

put you on firm ground.

Your life will be a song to Him.

The world will be amazed at God!

Your Father knows you inside and out.

He made you with His holy hands.

He embraces all of you—your "good" and your "bad." He's been with you every moment of your life.

Every hair is numbered.

They might be a mess, but they're numbered!

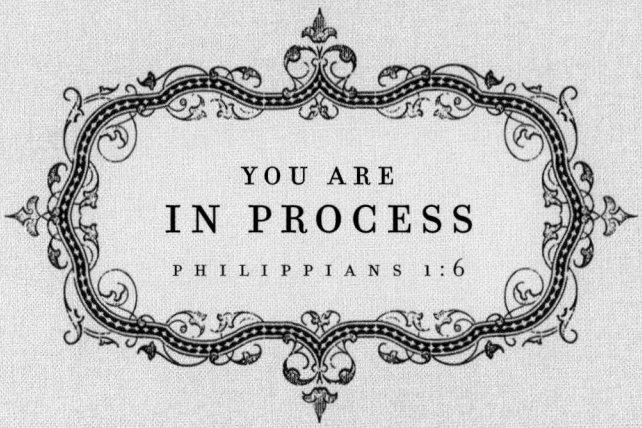

You are becoming perfected in Christ.

He's been working in you.

He will continue to mold and shape you.

The frustrations in your life

are His sandpaper.

Hold still and let Him do His job.

He knows exactly what He's doing.

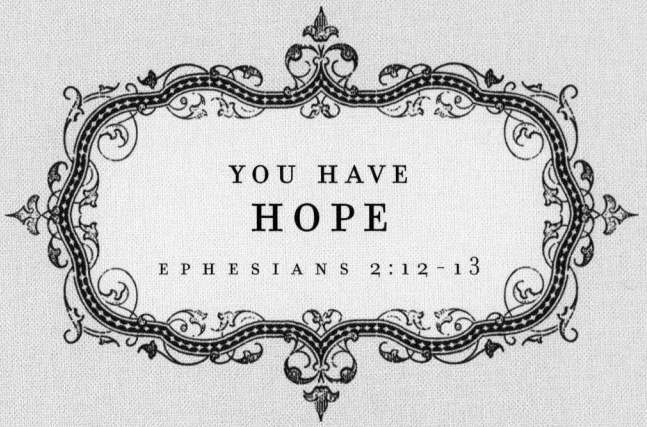

You have been bought with a price.

You are worth more than gold.

He sees you as His precious child.

Pray that He will open your eyes to that fact.

No good thing will He withhold from you.

Jesus made it all possible!

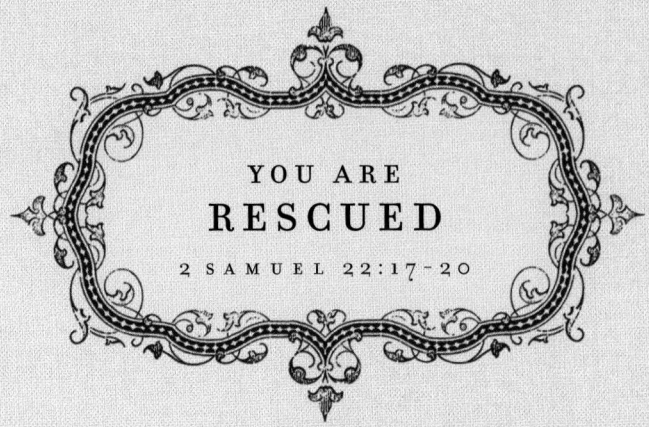

Your needs are not too much for God.

He holds all the earth in His control.

He sustains all of life.

It is not a frustration or a difficulty for Him to care for you.

He will give to you in abundance.

He wants to provide for you!

You have not been abandoned.

God has adopted you.

You, who were far away,

have been brought near.

He delights in the fact that you are His.

Yes, life is hard. And yes, you are His child!

He is your Daddy, Papa, Abba!

You are blessed and restored as you sleep.

He is carefully watching over you.

Rest in the fact that

His eyes are always on you.

Fall asleep knowing

He is restoring you in every way.

Sweet dreams!

You don't have to carry a burden of shame.

With God there is no condemnation.

You have been declared "not guilty."

Christ's righteousness is now yours.

He's the lifter of your head.

The chains of shame are cut. Now fly!

You are a new creation.

The old you is dying away.

The power of the Holy Spirit is your defense.

He is breaking the bonds of your past.

He's redeeming the years you've lost.

You are looking

more like your Father everyday!

You are precious.

You are a pearl of great price.

You have been declared righteous.

God paid a big price for you

and delights in your devotion to Him.

Your worth is beyond measure!

You are not alone.

He is next to you right now!

And He is always there

no matter where you go or what you do.

He continually offers you great hope!

Release all your worries and fears to Him.

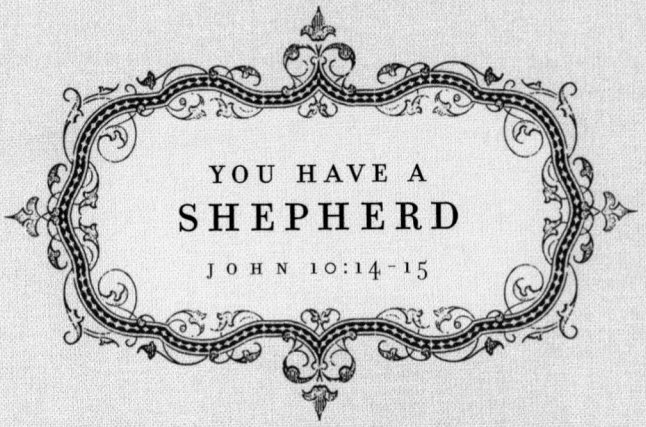

You are His sheep.

He's watching out for you.

He knows your tendency to wander.

Listen for His voice; He's calling to you.

Follow Him to the greenest grass.

You will be most satisfied in His presence.

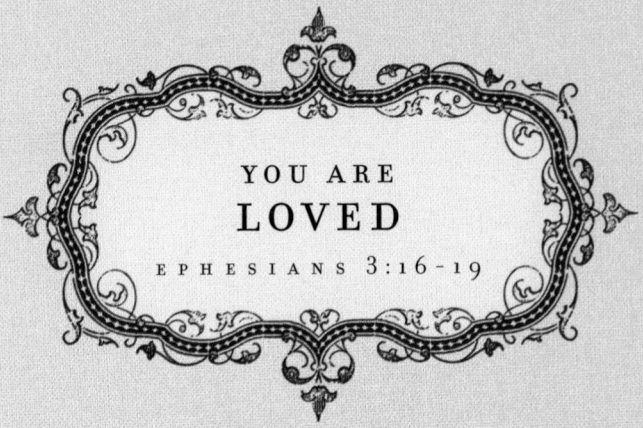

You are being strengthened in your innermost being.

You are being rooted and established in love. He is revealing His great love to you and for you. He is transforming your mind as you turn your thoughts to Him. You are given great hope and power as you trust in Him. Let the wind blow; you are firmly planted!

Your thoughts are not His thoughts.

Give your expectations of others and your circumstances over to Him. Let Him orchestrate all the details. His plans may not be your plans, but He sees the big picture. He knows the end of the story.

You are becoming like Him.

He is glorified as you focus on Him.

Your sufferings can bring Him glory.

He has experienced life like this too.

Especially in the hard times, He can shine through you.

That's a painful, yet beautiful, truth!

You can rest today.

He has it all under control.

You can give Him your "to-do" list.

He holds all time in His hands.

He is powerful and over all things.

Enjoy each moment.

The King is on His throne.

You are unique.

He made you very special.

You are not a mistake or a second thought.

You were planned by God.

Nothing was left out.

He delights in His creation of you.

Let Him see that big smile!

ALSO AVAILABLE

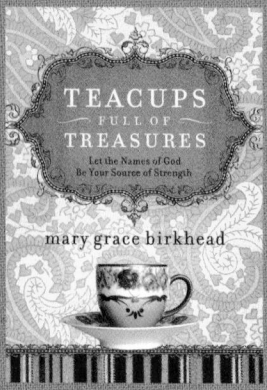

TEACUPS FULL OF TREASURES

ISBN 1-59145-495-6

As you catch glimpses of unique and lovely teacups, and the names and character of God, you will receive a warm invitation to sit comfortably with your Heavenly Father as you discover anew how much He loves you.

BEAUTIFULLY PINNED PROMISES

ISBN 1-59145-496-4

As you enjoy charming and sparkling heirlooms, and God's blessings from the Psalms, you will discover promises that touch your heart with grace, and that you can hold onto and call your own.

www.marygraceb.com

Available wherever books are sold.

INTEGRITY®
PUBLISHERS